Shades of Life

Dr. Rashid Gill

Dedication

To my beloved wife, Arina Gill —

the light in my darkness,

the strength in my weakness,

and the quiet grace that completes my soul.

Contents

Scattered Thoughts

My thoughts are scattered like dry leaves in fall,
They do not know their destiny or call.
Carried by winds to places unknown,
Drifting in silence, yet never alone.

Each leaf a whisper of dreams once near,
Now trembling softly, fragile with fear.
Yet in their wandering, beauty is found,
A quiet dance upon the ground.

And though they scatter, aimless, apart,
Each still belongs to the tree of my heart.

One day the breeze will guide them home,
No longer lost, no more to roam.

Rev. Dr. Rashid Gill

Life Is a Mystery

Life is a mystery; nobody can know,

Every day brings new tension and a blow.

We plan our steps, yet paths rearrange,

What we call certain may swiftly change.

Dreams take flight, yet falter mid-air,

Blessings arrive, yet burdened with care.

We chase tomorrow, forgetting today,

Losing the peace that could light our way.

Still in the struggle, wisdom is found,

Hope takes root in the roughest ground.

Each trial endured, though hidden in pain,

Leaves behind lessons that always remain.

The More We Try

The more we try, the less we gain,

Our striving often ends in pain.

We chase the heights, yet slip and fall,

For life gives little though we give all.

Desires grow faster than hands can keep,

Their promises fade, their roots run deep.

We build our castles on shifting sand,

Only to watch them leave our hand.

But hidden within the loss and strife,

Are lessons that carve the shape of life.

The heart grows wiser, the soul more strong,

When trials reveal where we belong.

So let us labor, but not despair,

For grace still answers the fervent prayer.

True gain is not in what we possess,

But peace of spirit and quiet blessedness.

Lessons of Life

The lessons we gain from life's long years,
Are often written in trials and tears.
Wisdom may come through struggle and strain,
Yet it is purchased with sorrow and pain.

Each step we take brings burdens to bear,
Each dream pursued is tangled with care.
We long for peace, yet heartache remains,
Etching its mark through losses and chains.

Yet pain refines, like fire through gold,
Revealing truths our hearts must hold.
Through storms endured, our spirits grow,
Finding a strength we never could know.

So though life's lessons may cut us deep,
Their hidden treasures are ours to keep.
Courage and hope through trials are given,
Guiding the soul on its way to heaven.

Love's Paradox

Love may build you, yet also destroy,

In destiny's hands, we are but toys.

It lifts the soul to heights untold,

Then casts it down, abandoned and cold.

It whispers softly, a tender song,

Yet burns with fire when things go wrong.

A balm for wounds, a source of strife,

Love is the paradox shaping life.

It crowns with joy, it wounds with tears,

It strengthens faith, yet awakens fears.

A fleeting gift, both bitter and sweet,

A path where sorrow and rapture meet.

Yet still we seek it, time after time,

For love gives meaning, both harsh and sublime.

Though fragile, fleeting, and bound by cost,

Without its flame, life's essence is lost.

Rev. Dr. Rashid Gill

Hard Work and Patience

Shortcut in life brings only loss and defeat,

Hard work and patience are steadfast; they never cheat.

I learned through trials, sorrow, and pain,

That fleeting ease leads only to chains.

Every effort, however small, shapes the soul,

Patience and diligence together make us whole.

Rushing ahead, ignoring the path,

Leaves hearts empty and dreams cut in half.

Those who envy shortcuts may seem to rise,

But their towers crumble before wise eyes.

Time rewards the steady, the faithful, the true,

Not fleeting luck that vanishes like morning dew.

So I walk carefully, guided by what I've known,

Through hard work, patience, and seeds I've sown.

Life is a journey, lessons earned through strife,

And every honest effort enriches life.

The Cost of Greed

Money can buy whatever one desires,

Yet leaves the soul empty, consumed by fires.

All other virtues seem to fade away,

When wealth alone dictates the day.

I chased its glitter, thought it would suffice,

But found no peace, only hidden vice.

The heart grows weary, the spirit confined,

True joy and honor are then hard to find.

Regret now whispers in the silent night,

Lessons learned through folly, wrong from right.

Virtue and kindness, love and grace,

Cannot be purchased, no wealth can replace.

So I turn my gaze from treasures untold,

Seeking the riches that cannot be sold.

For life's true wealth lies in hearts made free,

Not in gold or silver, but in integrity.

Rev. Dr. Rashid Gill

The Price of Beauty and Love

Beauty, sympathy, and love, always had their way,

They touched my heart deeply, yet led me astray.

What seemed so tender brought me hidden strife,

Lessons learned in shadows shaped the course of life.

I gave my heart freely, believing in their grace,

But pain followed swiftly, leaving no embrace.

Even joy turned fleeting, hope often betrayed,

By the very gifts I thought would never fade.

Yet through each sorrow, wisdom softly spoke,

Teaching me patience, the strength to evoke.

Not all that glimmers can heal or sustain,

Some charms conceal both pleasure and pain.

So now I cherish with care, I guard what is true,

Love and beauty are precious, but must be pursued with view.

Sympathy and passion, tempered by mind,

Bring peace to the heart, and serenity to find.

Scattered Thoughts

(Title to be added)

A woman stands where worlds collide,
Tradition's strength and modern pride.
She weaves the old into the new,
A tapestry of values true.

Her roots are deep, her branches wide,
She carries grace the times can't hide.
In modern roles she claims her voice,
Yet keeps her family's sacred choice.

She blends respect with freedom's song,
And proves the two can still belong.
Her wisdom shines, her love unites,
Her courage builds, her spirit lights.

So let the world its changes see,
She shows the path of harmony.
For in her hands the future lies,
Where values live and dreams can rise.

Rev. Dr. Rashid Gill

What the Broken Need

In sorrow's night when shadows stay,

Advice can chase all hope away.

A gentle word, a tender hand,

Is what the weary heart can stand.

The mind grows weak, the spirit worn,

The heart feels fragile, bruised, and torn.

Yet love can heal, and kindness mend,

Where lessons fail, compassion bends.

Too many speak, too few will hear,

Their counsel deepens pain and fear.

But one who listens, soft and true,

Can help the broken make it through.

So give no lecture, cold or long,

But let your presence be the song.

For sympathy, with love combined,

Will bring the peace a soul can find.

"Chance and Choice in Love"

Love comes by chance, or through our try,

A fleeting spark or a steady tie.

It's hard to build a bond that will stay,

Yet hearts keep reaching, finding their way.

Sometimes it blooms in the quiet unknown,

Other times, effort must make it grown.

Desire may pull, and care may guide,

But only patience keeps it alive.

Fate may open doors we never foresee,

Yet love requires both chance and decree.

A tender balance of heart and will,

Shapes the connection, quiet yet real.

Through joy and struggle, through loss and gain,

Love teaches wisdom from pleasure and pain.

It is both fragile and daringly strong,

A journey of hearts, where all belong.

Rev. Dr. Rashid Gill

"The Spark and the Bond"

Attraction is the spark that lights the way,

A natural pull we cannot disobey.

Though society may frown, and traditions may sigh,

It is a truth we cannot deny.

Desire may flare, intense and bright,

Lust burns fast in the depth of night.

Yet fleeting fire cannot alone sustain,

It fades unless love guides the flame.

Love grows slowly, built on care,

On trust, respect, and hearts laid bare.

Balance is knowing both are real,

And wisdom shapes the way we feel.

"In the Mist of Feelings"

In the mist of feelings, we lose our way,

Between love and lust, hearts often sway.

Is it nature's call or a sudden thrust,

A fragile heart torn between longing and trust?

Passion may blaze with a fleeting fire,

But love moves slowly, lifting higher.

One fades with time, one weathers the storm,

Guiding the soul, keeping the heart warm.

We chase what seems near, yet slips from our hand,

Confusing desire with love's true command.

The mind may falter, the heart may blind,

Yet in quiet thought, the truth we find.

So pause in the mist, let your senses see,

What is fleeting, and what is meant to be.

For love is steady, enduring, and real,

Not just the spark that passion can steal.

Rev. Dr. Rashid Gill

After a long while!

Ater a long while, I broke the relation,

Which never existed in fact.

This is the story of my love,

And of life's cunning tact.

I walked with a dream that was never real,

A shadowed bond I could not feel.

Love was a whisper, faint and concealed,

Yet it pierced my heart with steel.

The silence echoed where words should be,

A tie unformed still wounded me.

Life in its wisdom let me see,

What love is — and what is not to be.

Now with the truth I stand refined,

Leaving illusions far behind.

Love may deceive, but life is kind,

It carves new strength within the mind.

Held

Time and tide move on — they will not wait or stay;

I stand against their hurry, and keep my breath at bay.

The world may turn its back, and doubts may crowd the door,

Yet what I place within your hands I guard forevermore.

Not blind with restless trust, nor naive with easy praise,

But practised in the quiet, through nights and tangled days.

I give you what grows silent when the clamor starts to roar —

A thing both small and sacred, something I could guard no more.

So take it, careful stranger, and hold it as you choose;

I'll not demand your promise nor burden you with dues.

If time should steal the daylight and the tides forget to stay,

This flicker I have handed you will keep the dark away.

Rev. Dr. Rashid Gill

The Name That Remains

In the book of my heart, every line is filled with your name,
Written in whispers of love, like an unending flame.
The ink may fade on other words, or vanish with time,
But your name endures — eternal, steadfast, sublime.

The world around keeps changing, new faces come and go,
Yet one name shines brighter than all I could ever know.
Like the sun through the shadows, it pierces through the haze,
Guiding me gently through life's uncertain maze.

When storms rise within me, and my courage feels small,
Your name is the anchor that steadies it all.
A shelter unbroken, a light that won't depart,
It beats like a rhythm deep inside my heart.

So let kingdoms crumble and the stars lose their flame,
Still the song of my soul will echo your name.
Though all else may wither and vanish away,
Your name is my treasure, forever to stay.

"Through It All"

Though both of us reached for the dreams in our hands,
We stumbled and faltered, despite all our plans.

Through storms and through shadows, together we tried,
Yet the road would not yield, no matter how wide.

Still, every setback, each tear and each fall,
Bore the quiet reminder: we gave it our all.

And though the end lingered just out of our view,
The strength of our journey was born between two.

Rev. Dr. Rashid Gill

"The Radiance of Her Years"

Her face glows gently, a candle in night,

A presence of comfort, a soft, steady light.

With frankness she speaks, yet her silence is sweet,

A blend of shy grace and a spirit complete.

Her beauty is tender, yet brilliant and rare,

A wisdom that sparkles, a charm beyond compare.

As soft as the whisper of thoughts yet unspoken,

She carries within her a heart never broken.

In the bloom of her thirties, her vigour shines through,

With dreams yet to blossom, with skies ever blue.

To sit in her presence is joy's recompense—

A union of beauty, of brilliance, of sense.

The Cost of Wealth

Nowadays a man is known by gold,

By how much wealth his hands can hold.

Yet in this chase for shining gain,

Morality suffers, hearts feel pain.

Wealth may tempt, may blind, may bind,

Corrupting thought and clouding mind.

The greed that grows within the chest

Can rob the soul and steal the rest.

Riches rise, yet values fall,

Humanity silenced by the call.

For what is gained at virtue's cost

Leaves deeper wounds than fortune lost.

So let us measure not by gold,

But by the love and truth we hold.

For wealth may glitter, but cannot keep

The soul intact, the conscience deep.

Rev. Dr. Rashid Gill

Against Might

In many cases, they say, "Might is right,"
A shadow cast on truth and light.
But I cannot bow, cannot comply,
For justice calls, and I must try.

Power may press, the strong may reign,
Yet conscience speaks through loss and pain.
I stand resolved, though storms assail,
For right must rise, and truth prevail.

Against the tide, against the force,
I choose the steadfast, honest course.
Though fear may whisper, doubt may bite,
I lift my voice, defend the right.

So let the world wield strength and sway,
I will not yield, I will not stay.
For honor guides where might may roam,
And courage fights to bring truth home.

Gentle Silence

I do not speak the truth to her face,

Perhaps I choose to let it embrace.

For in my silence, a comfort flows,

Easing the tension she rarely shows.

Sometimes the heart must weigh its words,

Not every truth must be heard.

A gentle lie, or quiet refrain,

Can soften sorrow, lessen the pain.

Yet in this act, a choice is made,

A balance between honesty and aid.

To shield, to care, to let it be,

Sometimes silence speaks more gently.

So I remain, unseen, unknown,

A guardian of peace, quietly shown.

Though truth may hide in subtle art,

The heart can guide a loving part.

Rev. Dr. Rashid Gill

One True Friend

No matter how many friends you find,

There's only one close to your mind.

The rest appear, then fade away,

Like fleeting thoughts that cannot stay.

Some bring laughter, some bring cheer,

Yet leave when shadows draw near.

Their presence fades, their echoes die,

Like passing clouds in a restless sky.

But one remains, steadfast and true,

A guiding light when storms pursue.

Through trials, joy, and quiet days,

Their love endures in countless ways.

So treasure well that chosen heart,

For from the start, it sets apart.

Amid the many, they alone remain,

A constant in life's shifting lane.

Like Morning Dew

Each day I fall more in love with you,

You touch my heart as gentle as dew.

A quiet grace at the break of dawn,

A tender light I lean upon.

Your presence glows, serene and bright,

A guiding star through the darkest night.

Like dew on petals, soft and true,

My soul finds peace when held by you.

In fleeting moments, love takes flight,

Turning shadows into morning light.

No force on earth can tear apart

The sacred bond within my heart.

So let each day renew its song,

In your embrace, I still belong.

With every breath, my spirit knows,

Like morning dew, our love still grows.

Rev. Dr. Rashid Gill

Spirit and Soul

We are together like spirit and soul,
Two halves united, one perfect whole.
Love is hidden, yet steady and near,
A silent strength that conquers fear.

It rests within us, calm and deep,
A sacred treasure the heart must keep.
Like water contained in a vessel still,
Love flows gently, by Heaven's will.

No storm can break, no fire consume,
The bond we share, it will not doom.
For spirit and soul in harmony stay,
Guiding our steps along life's way.

So let this love in silence grow,
As rivers beneath the surface flow.
In spirit and soul, our lives entwine,
A lasting truth, both yours and mine.

The Blind Well

My heart is like a deep blind well,

I draw my thoughts from it to tell.

Silent waters, dark and still,

Hold secrets shaped by time and will.

Each echo rises from depths unknown,

Whispers not mine, yet all my own.

Truth concealed in shadows deep,

Awakens when the soul can weep.

A hidden spring of joy and pain,

Of fleeting loss and lasting gain.

The world may see but not discern,

The depths from which my visions burn.

So let me draw, though blind I be,

The living words that flow in me.

For from this well, both vast and true,

Emerge the thoughts I give to you.

Rev. Dr. Rashid Gill

Love by Divine Will

Falling in love with you was never my plan,

It was the will of God, not the choice of man.

A path unseen, yet clearly shown,

A seed of grace divinely sown.

Not by desire, nor fleeting flame,

But by His hand, this union came.

Through twists of fate, through trials near,

God's gentle voice has brought me here.

Love such as this no storm can break,

For heaven guards the steps we take.

What man designs may fade away,

But God's own will shall ever stay.

So I cherish this bond, both deep and true,

Ordained by heaven, between me and you.

A sacred gift, a holy sign,

Your heart in mine, by God's design.

The Untold Heart

Love can make the strongest heart refrain,
A silent battle, a hidden pain.
Courage retreats where feelings swell,
A secret story no tongue will tell.

Beneath the smiles, behind the eyes,
Lie whispered truths, concealed cries.
We mask our fear, we hide our dreams,
Yet hope persists in quiet streams.

The world judges what it cannot see,
Blind to the depth of vulnerability.
But hearts that tremble, yet still endure,
Reveal a strength both soft and pure.

So speak your truth, though fear is near,
For hidden hearts deserve to hear.
In honesty lies courage profound,
Where love and fear are tightly bound.

Rev. Dr. Rashid Gill

Shared Struggles

I tried to confess my hidden pain,

Hoping my voice was not in vain.

Perhaps there are others who feel the same,

Silent souls caught in life's harsh game.

In crowded streets, in empty rooms,

Many hearts bear unseen dooms.

Yet fear of judgment keeps us still,

Trapped by shadows against our will.

But sharing truth can light the way,

Connecting hearts that often sway.

In knowing others feel our plight,

We find compassion, strength, and light.

So I speak softly, yet with intent,

Hoping my words are not misspent.

For in our struggles, shared and known,

We build a bridge, we're not alone.

Hidden Truths

I feel something strange dwelling in me,
A secret I hide, never truly free.
Though I speak in words, my heart conceals,
The silent pain my soul reveals.

Behind each smile, behind each gaze,
A hidden truth winds through life's maze.
I long for courage to let it show,
To face myself, to let others know.

Yet fear holds tight, a shadowed chain,
Whispering doubts, fueling the strain.
Still in the quiet, I search for the key,
To break these bonds and finally be.

So one day soon, I hope to find,
The strength to speak, to free my mind.
For truth embraced, though slow it starts,
Can heal the wounds of hidden hearts.

Rev. Dr. Rashid Gill

Broken Dreams

In the mist of doubts and snares,

My dreams lie shattered; no one cares.

Yet still I rise, though hearts may fail,

Through stormy nights and winds that wail.

Each fragment holds a story untold,

Of hope once bright, of courage bold.

Though shadows linger, I seek the light,

Guiding my soul through endless night.

The world may turn, indifferent, cold,

But inner strength begins to unfold.

From broken pieces, I build anew,

A path of purpose, steadfast and true.

So though my dreams were torn apart,

I carry courage within my heart.

For in each trial, each silent scream,

I find the spark to chase my dream.

Stand Tall

I want to stay honest, true to me,
To friends, to foes, to all who see.
No mask I wear, no hidden guise,
My heart speaks openly, no disguise.

In the company of sages and magids wise,
I stand with courage, head held high.
Through whispers of doubt and shadows near,
I walk with purpose, without fear.

Integrity guides me, a steady flame,
Through fleeting praise or passing shame.
Each step I take, each choice I make,
Reflects the path I will not forsake.

So let the world judge, let whispers call,
I rise unwavering, I stand tall.
For in my truth, my soul takes flight,
A beacon of honor, in day and night.

Rev. Dr. Rashid Gill

Moments So Rare

In all the circumstances, suspicions, and fears,

I stand with courage, through doubts and tears.

Though shadows may gather and storms may flare,

I hold my heart, for such moments are rare.

When whispers of worry cloud the mind,

And truths seem hidden, impossible to find,

I search within, where hope quietly grows,

A steadfast light that only the brave know.

Through trials unending, and nights so long,

I discover strength I thought was gone.

Each heartbeat reminds me of life's gentle care,

That even in darkness, such moments are rare.

So cherish the fleeting, the tender, the true,

The glimpses of love that break through the blue.

In a world of chaos, let your spirit prepare,

To embrace with wonder, for these moments are rare.

Journey of the Heart

The journey of the heart is long,

A winding path, both weak and strong.

Through joys and sorrows, hopes and fears,

It travels onward through the years.

Each step it takes, each beat it gives,

Shapes the life that each heart lives.

Through love and loss, it learns to bend,

And finds new ways to start again.

The heart's journey never ends,

It twists, it turns, it always mends.

Through every trial, every part,

We grow, we learn—the heart's own art.

Through every sunrise, through every night,

It finds its courage, embraces the light.

A story written in beats and sighs,

The heart endures, and love never dies.

Rev. Dr. Rashid Gill

Strength in Silence

In quiet strength, my soul persists,

Amidst the chaos, it insists.

No need for noise, no need for fame,

True power lies without a name.

Through silent trials, courage grows,

A steady stream that gently flows.

It bends, it sways, yet never breaks,

The strength within that life awakes.

No clamor can disturb the heart,

No shallow praise can play a part.

In calm resolve, in silent might,

We find our strength, our guiding light.

Moments Unseen

Moments unseen, yet deeply felt,

In every heart, emotions melt.

A fleeting glance, a subtle sign,

Shapes our journey, redefines.

The silent touch, the whispered thought,

In these small things, life is caught.

Invisible threads that bind and weave,

A tapestry only hearts perceive.

Though unnoticed, their power is true,

Creating paths we never knew.

So cherish the unseen, embrace the small,

For in these moments, we find it all.

Rev. Dr. Rashid Gill

Fire Within

A fire burns, unseen, untamed,

Through every struggle, unashamed.

It fuels my dreams, it lights my way,

Through darkest night, through brightest day.

It whispers courage, it shouts desire,

A relentless force, an inner fire.

Through fear and doubt, it guides my hand,

And gives me strength to boldly stand.

No wind can quench, no storm can sway,

This fire within will always stay.

A beacon bright, it never fades,

Through life's complexities and shades.

Eternal Bond

Our bond eternal, through time and space,

No power can alter, no force erase.

Through laughter and tears, through joy and pain,

Our hearts entwined, a sacred chain.

No storm can sever, no night divide,

For love eternal will still abide.

A promise kept beyond all measure,

A cherished soul, a treasured treasure.

Through fleeting years, our spirits soar,

Bound together forevermore.

In every heartbeat, in every sigh,

Our eternal bond will never die.

Rev. Dr. Rashid Gill

Silent Whispers

Silent whispers call my name,

Through winds of change, they remain the same.

Messages soft, yet deeply profound,

In every corner, their echoes resound.

They speak of hope, they speak of grace,

Of hidden paths we all must face.

Though quiet, their power cannot hide,

A guiding force, forever beside.

Through doubt and fear, their words appear,

Comforting hearts, calming fear.

A gentle nudge, a tender plea,

To open eyes and truly see.

So listen close, to whispers near,

They carry wisdom, they carry cheer.

In quiet moments, truths unfold,

Silent whispers, treasures untold.

Shadows and Light

We walk between shadows and light,

Through silent mornings and restless nights.

Life's journey tests our strength and will,

Yet hope remains, enduring still.

In every shadow, a lesson lies,

A spark of wisdom, a new sunrise.

Through darkest paths, our hearts are tried,

Yet courage blooms, we shall not hide.

The light returns, as sure as rain,

Healing sorrow, softening pain.

Through tears and laughter, joy and strife,

We find the balance that shapes our life.

So hold your head high, embrace the fight,

Both shadows and light make the world bright.

In every struggle, in every gleam,

We realize the truth of our dream.

Rev. Dr. Rashid Gill

Longing Heart

I long for you, the need of my soul,

Without your love, I am not whole.

A fire within, both fierce and bright,

Burning through day, consuming night.

Your touch, your voice, your gentle gaze,

Sets my weary heart ablaze.

In your absence, I feel the ache,

Yet through the longing, I never break.

Each heartbeat calls your sacred name,

A love eternal, a steady flame.

Through distance, time, and endless trial,

I hold your essence all the while.

And when we meet, the world aligns,

Our hearts entwined, our fates combined.

Longing fulfilled, the soul takes flight,

Bathing in love's pure light.

Your Grace is Sufficient

Your grace is sufficient for all I face,
A boundless river of love and grace.
Through every struggle, every fight,
Your mercy shines, a guiding light.

When shadows threaten and fears arise,
I lift my heart, I close my eyes.
For in your care, I find my way,
Through darkest night and brightest day.

No power on earth can take away,
The peace you grant, come what may.
Through trials and storms, I stand tall,
Your grace sufficient, encompassing all.

Forever in awe, my soul shall sing,
Of mercy, love, and hope you bring.
In every breath, in every call,
Your grace sustains me through it all.

Rev. Dr. Rashid Gill

You Are My Refuge

When storms arise and shadows fall,

You are my refuge through it all.

A shelter strong against the night,

A beacon guiding with steady light.

No fear can linger, no doubt can stay,

For you protect me along my way.

Your love, a fortress, ever near,

Dispels the darkness, calms my fear.

Through trials, troubles, and despair,

I find my solace in your care.

A place of peace where I belong,

Your presence turns my weak to strong.

So in your arms, I safely rest,

With hope renewed and spirit blessed.

Forever faithful, ever true,

My refuge, my strength, my love is you.

In the Rain of Tears

In the rain of my tears, my sighs are burning,
A heart that's restless, always yearning.
Yet through the storm, I find my way,
Guided by hope, I face the day.

Each droplet holds a story untold,
Of dreams deferred and hands grown cold.
Yet in this rain, a strength I see,
A deeper sense of what life can be.

The sky may weep, yet so do I,
Letting emotions freely fly.
Through grief and loss, I rise again,
Cleansed by sorrow, freed from pain.

And when the sun breaks through the gray,
It warms my soul in a gentle way.
The rain of tears becomes my song,
A melody carrying me along.

Rev. Dr. Rashid Gill

The Flow of Life

Every moment of life flows like water,

Try to stop it, it moves even faster.

We grasp at time, yet it slips away,

Guiding us gently, come what may.

Rivers of moments, both bitter and sweet,

Carry our laughter, our defeats.

We bend, we break, yet rise anew,

The current carries both me and you.

Life's lessons come with patient grace,

Each ripple and wave, a sacred place.

In stillness, we find the depth we seek,

In movement, the courage to be unique.

So let the river of life sweep through,

Embrace each wave, both old and new.

Scattered Thoughts

For in the flow, our hearts are free,

Carved by time, like a deep, vast sea.

Rev. Dr. Rashid Gill

You Are My Soul

I am your body, you are my soul,

Without your love, I am not whole.

You are the flame that lights my way,

The breath I need with every day.

Your touch consumes, your whispers heal,

A bond so sacred, a love so real.

Through trials, triumphs, joy, and pain,

With you, my heart shall ever remain.

No distance, no time can us divide,

For in your love, I shall reside.

Each heartbeat echoes our shared song,

Together we rise, forever strong.

So hold my hand, don't let it go,

Our spirits entwined, our love will grow.

Scattered Thoughts

In body and soul, we find our goal,

I am your body, you are my soul.

Rev. Dr. Rashid Gill

Hope in Dismay

There is hope even in my dismay,

You are with me, night and day.

When clouds obscure the brightest skies,

Your presence lifts and fortifies.

Through every sorrow, every tear,

I feel your comfort always near.

Though life may break, and paths may bend,

Your love and grace will never end.

A song melodious, tender, and true,

Flows from my heart because of you.

Even when shadows try to claim,

Your light within remains the same.

Intensity

Intensity burns within my chest,

A restless fire that will not rest.

Passion and longing weave through my days,

In quiet moments and in loud displays.

The heart races, the mind takes flight,

Through darkest valleys, into light.

Every glance, every whispered word,

A symphony felt, yet barely heard.

I chase the shadows, embrace the sun,

In endless battle, never undone.

Life's every rhythm, every chance,

Moves me forward in this dance.

Intensity shapes the path I tread,

A river of feelings, alive, widespread.

I surrender to its call and its flow,

For only in intensity do I truly know.

You Are My Gain

You are the purpose of my life and gain,

My comfort in sorrow, my relief in pain.

With every dawn, your light I see,

A guiding star that sets me free.

In silent moments, your voice I hear,

A melody gentle, ever near.

Through storms and trials, you hold my hand,

With you beside me, I firmly stand.

The world may tremble, yet I remain,

Anchored by love through joy and strain.

No fleeting pleasure can compare,

To the peace you give beyond despair.

Forever bound by heart and soul,

You make my broken pieces whole.

In every tear, in every smile,

Your love accompanies every mile.

Your Love Flows

Your love flows in me like blood in veins,

Hidden within me, through joys and pains.

A force unseen yet felt so deep,

A treasure within I long to keep.

Through silent nights and brightest day,

Your presence guides me on my way.

Even in shadows, I feel your light,

Turning the darkness into sight.

The heart may falter, yet love remains,

Through all losses, through all gains.

It whispers softly, yet loudly calls,

Breaking my fences, tearing down walls.

Rev. Dr. Rashid Gill

Reality of Life

Reality of life, we often hide,

Shy away with pride, though pain resides.

Moments slip by, like rivers they flow,

Yet courage and truth help us to grow.

To teach a heart to be bold and free,

Is a virtue worth more than gold, you see.

Life's harsh lessons, both bitter and sweet,

Shape our souls and make us complete.

We stumble, we fall, yet rise once more,

Learning the truths we had ignored before.

Through shadows and light, our paths align,

With hope and wisdom as our sign.

So face the world, let honesty reign,

Embrace the joy, endure the pain.

Scattered Thoughts

Each heartbeat echoes what we become,

Life's reality, both tender and glum.

Rev. Dr. Rashid Gill

Thorns Among Roses

It is said a life is shaped by the company it keeps,

Yet truth is more stubborn, it cuts and it weeps.

I have watched thorns dwell where the fair roses grow,

Still sharp in their nature, still quick to bestow.

A kind soul may blossom when touched by the kind,

While cold hearts stay hardened, unmoved in their mind.

Not every neighbor of beauty learns grace—

Some bear the garden, yet poison its space.

So walk with the wise, let their counsel refine,

Let hearts that are gentle grow woven with thine.

But learn this truth, wherever you roam:

A thorn stays a thorn, though it lives in a home.

And thus we discern, in each path that we choose,

The friends we embrace are the virtues we lose.

Scattered Thoughts

Seek light for your soul, let dark company cease—

For flowers bring fragrance, but thorns steal your peace.

Rev. Dr. Rashid Gill

Chance and Choice in Love

Love comes by chance, or through our try,

A fleeting spark or a steady tie.

It's hard to build a bond that will stay,

Yet hearts keep reaching, finding their way.

Sometimes it blooms in the quiet unknown,

Other times, effort must make it grown.

Desire may pull, and care may guide,

But only patience keeps it alive.

Fate may open doors we never foresee,

Yet love requires both chance and decree.

A tender balance of heart and will,

Shapes the connection, quiet yet real.

Through joy and struggle, through loss and gain,

Love teaches wisdom from pleasure and pain.

Scattered Thoughts

It is both fragile and daringly strong,

A journey of hearts, where all belong.

Rev. Dr. Rashid Gill

The Spark and the Bond

Attraction is the spark that lights the way,

A natural pull we cannot disobey.

Though society may frown, and traditions may sigh,

It is a truth we cannot deny.

Desire may flare, intense and bright,

Lust burns fast in the depth of night.

Yet fleeting fire cannot alone sustain,

It fades unless love guides the flame.

Love grows slowly, built on care,

On trust, respect, and hearts laid bare.

Balance is knowing both are real,

And wisdom shapes the way we feel.

Learning in Pain

Mistakes are teachers, harsh but true,

Dressed in shadows, yet showing you.

Each stumble hurts, each fall may sting,

But from the hurt, new strength will spring.

The path is jagged, the journey long,

Yet every misstep hums a song.

It whispers softly, "Rise once more,"

And opens windows you've not seen before.

Hurt is heavy, and tears may flow,

Yet they water seeds you'll someday grow.

Pain is the tutor we cannot refuse,

It carves the heart and hones our muse.

So welcome mistakes, though they may bite,

For they turn the darkness into light.

Every scar, every tear you gain,

Becomes a bridge from loss to reign.

My Possessions

The hurts, wounds, sorrows and pains,

These are my possessions; these are my gains.

Life carves its lessons with a ruthless hand,

Leaving marks no soul can fully understand.

I gather the tears that fall in the night,

They glimmer as jewels in a hidden light.

Though the world may scorn what I hold inside,

These scars are the proof of battles survived.

Each burden I carry has shaped who I am,

Each loss has refined me, like fire through sand.

Strength is not born in ease or delight,

But rises from ashes that darken the night.

So I will not curse what time has bestowed,

For pain is the lantern that lights my road.

Treasures may vanish, but one truth remains:

My soul is enriched by sorrows and pains.

Diamond and Destiny

Talent is a diamond, yet it needs luck to gleam,

Born from effort, polished by dream.

Shadows may fall, storms may confine,

Still it waits for its moment to shine.

Nothing truly belongs, nothing is mine,

Life lends its treasures, then draws the line.

We hold but a moment, a fleeting sign,

Of gifts and glories that intertwine.

Luck is the spark that ignites the flame,

Effort alone does not earn the fame.

Yet those who strive through night and pain,

See diamonds sparkle after the rain.

So I toil with heart, though fate may sway,

Grateful for each bright and fleeting day.

Talent and chance in a delicate dance,

Life gives the stage; we take the chance.

The Gift of Wounds

Wounds and hurts are gifts life gives for free,

Each pain a seed, each scar a tree.

Tears may fall, yet roots grow deep,

Wisdom blooms from the sorrows we keep.

Pain carves paths where courage can tread,

Turns silent fears into words unsaid.

From broken moments, strength will rise,

A soul reborn beneath stormy skies.

Scars are banners of battles won,

Proof that night surrenders to the sun.

Every ache, a teacher wise,

Shaping hearts that refuse disguise.

Life's cruel gifts are not in vain,

Through wounds and hurts, we break the chain.

Rev. Dr. Rashid Gill

What once was weakness now stands free,

A soul transformed, a mighty tree."

Life Is a Mystery

Life is a mystery; none can know,

Each day brings tension, trial, or blow.

We plan our path, yet shadows rearrange,

What feels so certain may suddenly change.

Dreams take flight but falter mid-air,

Joys arrive, yet are burdened with care.

We chase tomorrow, forgetting today,

Losing the peace that could light our way.

Yet in the struggle, wisdom is found,

Hope takes root in the hardest ground.

Each trial endured, though hidden in pain,

Leaves behind truths that always remain.

So let us journey with courage and trust,

Though life is fleeting, fragile as dust.

The mystery deepens, yet faith makes it clear,

Love is the compass that keeps us near.

Her Beauty

Her face was shining like the morning light,

Her smile was gentle, her eyes so bright.

She walked in silence, pure and free,

An angel of love, a dream to me.

Her laughter rang like a silver bell,

A melody sweet no words can tell.

Her tender steps, so soft, so kind,

She left a trace of heaven behind.

Her innocence glowed in all she did,

A treasure no jewel could ever bid.

Her beauty flowed like a golden stream,

She was my song, my heart, my dream.

Rev. Dr. Rashid Gill

Song: Treasure I Keep

Stanza 1

Your love fills me with rare happiness so deep,

This is the treasure I long to keep.

No gold, no jewels could shine so bright,

You are my joy, my soul's delight.

Chorus (catchy & simple)

You're my treasure, you're my song,

In your love is where I belong.

Stanza 2

Your voice is gentle, steady and true,

Each beat of my heart is singing for you.

Through storms and shadows, you light my way,

With you beside me, night turns to day.

Scattered Thoughts

Chorus

You're my treasure, you're my song,

In your love is where I belong.

Bridge

The world may change, the years may fly,

But love like ours will never die.

Rev. Dr. Rashid Gill

Love and Pride!

Stanza 1

My ego fights with love each day,

One pulls me close, one turns away.

If pride must win, then love must fade,

And I'm the prisoner both have made.

Stanza 2

I build my walls, then call it peace,

But love still cries for sweet release.

I long to hold what I let go,

Yet fear won't let my weakness show.

Stanza 3

The nights are cold, the silence deep,

My restless heart forgets to sleep.

For every tear my pride concealed,

Love counts the scars that time revealed.

Stanza 4

At last I see through all the pain,

That pride destroys what hearts could gain.

So let love rise, and ego fall,

For only love can conquer all.

Rev. Dr. Rashid Gill

Bitter or Better

One word can make life bitter or better,

A flame can warm or burn the letter.

A gentle heart can heal the pain,

A careless tongue can leave a stain.

The road we walk is ours to tread,

By what we've spoken, done, or said.

If kindness rules, our hearts grow lighter,

The darkest night turns somehow brighter.

When tempers rise and pride takes hold,

Our bitter tales are soon retold.

But when we choose the path of grace,

Peace and joy take sorrow's place.

So watch your words, both now and ever,

They shape your world for worse or better.

Life can be sweet or hard to bear—

The choice is ours, so handle with care.

The Fuel of Life

Life can be kind or can be cruel,

Yet faith within becomes our fuel.

When hope runs low and dreams seem far,

It's faith that lights our guiding star.

The storms may rise, the winds may shout,

But inner trust will drown the doubt.

Though shadows fall and tempests roar,

The heart believes — and asks no more.

We lose, we rise, we start anew,

Each wound reveals a brighter view.

The road is long, the steps are slow,

But faith keeps burning, soft and low.

So guard the flame that warms your soul,

Let courage keep your spirit whole.

For life can bruise, yet still be kind,

To those who keep their faith in mind.

Rev. Dr. Rashid Gill

A Better Life

We can live a better life,

If we stop judging others' strife.

Every heart has a tale untold,

Of dreams once warm, now turning cold.

Before you speak, take one more glance,

At someone lost in life's small dance.

A single smile, a word of grace,

Can light the dark in any place.

No one's flawless, none are pure,

We're all just souls who must endure.

Forgive the faults, release the pain,

And love will bloom through every chain.

So let your heart be soft, not proud,

Be gentle, even when it's loud.

For peace begins when hearts unite —

And judging ends where love takes flight.

Life Has Shown.

Life has shown that pain we must bear,

With patient hearts and earnest care.

Through storms we walk, through loss we grow,

For only pain can strength bestow.

When nights are long and hopes grow dim,

We learn to place our trust in Him.

Each tear that falls, each prayer that's said,

Becomes the light by which we're led.

The road is rough, the climb is steep,

Yet promises of faith we keep.

For every wound and every scar,

Reveal how strong we truly are.

So let us live with hearts made pure,

Through trials we stand, through pain endure.

For joy will come, though sorrow stays —

There's peace beyond these fleeting days.

Rev. Dr. Rashid Gill

What Life Taught Me

Life has taught me — nothing comes free,

Every dream demands a fee.

Pain and struggle carve the way,

Yet hope still whispers, "You'll be okay."

Charity taught me the joy of giving,

That love is the true art of living.

A gentle word, a helping hand,

Can heal a heart more than we planned.

Success once seemed a shining crown,

But time has slowly stripped it down.

Now I know, it's peace of mind,

That's hardest lost and rare to find.

I've learned to walk through storm and sun,

To lose with grace, when days are done.

For every scar and every tear,

Has made my vision sharp and clear.

Life's not about what we possess,

But what we share in tenderness.

To live, to give, to understand —

That's the mark of a life well-planned.

Rev. Dr. Rashid Gill

The Art of Living

There is an art to smile through pain,

Each wound we bear becomes our gain.

The trials faced, the tears we hide,

Are teachers walking by our side.

We chase the sun, we lose our way,

Yet learn from night what words can't say.

For every fall, for every scar,

Reveals how strong we truly are.

I've learned that peace is seldom loud,

It blooms within, not in the crowd.

True joy is simple, calm, and deep,

A promise even storms can't keep.

Now I don't seek a perfect road,

But strength to bear life's shifting load.

For pain and joy are threads the same —

Both weave the fabric of my name.

Treasures of the Simple Heart

Simplicity and contentment bring peace to life,

Desiring more than we need invites only strife.

A quiet heart, a steady mind,

Reveals the treasures most don't find.

The world may chase what glitters bright,

But fleeting gold can't hold the light.

True wealth is measured not by gain,

But by the calm that soothes the pain.

Small joys — a smile, a hand held tight,

A morning sun, the soft twilight.

These humble gifts, though simple and small,

Are worth far more than riches or hall.

Learn to let go of needless greed,

And plant the seeds that hearts truly need.

For in restraint, the spirit soars,

And life, at last, opens its doors.

Rev. Dr. Rashid Gill

Endless Worries

There is no end to worries and despairs,

They linger quietly in all our affairs.

Like shadows cast, they never sleep,

A burden carried, silent, deep.

Each day begins with hope anew,

Yet trials rise, as trials do.

The mind is restless, the heart unsure,

For every joy holds fears obscure.

But in these storms, the soul may grow,

Through pain, through doubt, through ebb and flow.

For strength is born where sorrows tread,

And light breaks forth where tears are shed.

So though life weaves its heavy chain,

We learn through loss, through grief, through pain.

For hope still shines, though faint, though far,

A guiding flame, a steadfast star.

The Cage of Desire

Desire is a cage, though it wears a smile,

It tempts the heart, deceives awhile.

It whispers freedom, boundless flight,

Yet chains the soul with hidden might.

Man builds his palace, proud and grand,

But finds no peace in wealth or land.

The more he gathers, the less he owns,

A slave enthroned upon his throne.

Desire consumes, it blinds the eyes,

It turns the truth to fleeting lies.

The fire it feeds will never cease,

Till wisdom learns the art of peace.

True freedom blooms when wants grow still,

When heart aligns with higher will.

For only then the soul can sing,

Unchained, unbound—a sovereign king.

Rev. Dr. Rashid Gill

Destiny's Path

What is our destiny, what is our fate?

No one can master it, early or late.

It weaves unseen, a hidden thread,

A road we walk, by heaven led.

We plan, we strive, we dream, we try,

Yet fate may change in the blink of an eye.

A twist, a turn, beyond our sight,

Can shift the day, can steal the night.

But though we cannot rule its hand,

We choose with heart where we will stand.

For courage still can shape the way,

And faith can brighten the darkest day.

So let fate write its secret song,

We walk with hope, we move along.

For though its mystery none can see,

We live with trust in what will be.

The Chains of Love

In love, we become a slave to one,

A truth of life that can't be shun.

The heart surrenders, the will is weak,

A silent vow the soul will keep.

It binds with cords both soft and tight,

A gentle cage, a sweet delight.

Though freedom fades, the heart still sings,

Content to serve, to wear love's rings.

Some call it loss, some call it gain,

For joy walks close beside the pain.

Yet in this bond, both strong and true,

We find a self both old and new.

So love enslaves, yet sets us free,

A paradox of destiny.

In chains we walk, yet gladly move,

For none escape the chains of love.

Rev. Dr. Rashid Gill

The Price of Living

Money is vital, of need and of strife,

It weighs even more in the bond of a wife.

For dreams are costly, and peace must be bought,

Each comfort earned, each blessing sought.

The bills arise, the burdens grow,

A husband learns what wages show.

The world may mock, yet truth is clear,

Money shapes much of love we hold dear.

But wealth alone can never sustain,

Without respect, all gold is vain.

For hearts need care, and souls need light,

Not only treasures counted at night.

So balance holds the truest way,

Let love guide wealth, not wealth betray.

Scattered Thoughts

For money may serve, but life is more,

A richer wealth than coins can store.

Rev. Dr. Rashid Gill

Shades of Life

Life is a complex; it has many shades,

A dance of the sunlight, a march through the shades.

Moments of laughter, moments of tears,

A story unfolding through countless years.

Time keeps moving, it carries us on,

Morning has vanished, evening has gone.

Yet scars remain, though hidden deep,

The soul still whispers what wounds still keep.

Each shade of life reveals its art,

A lesson carved upon the heart.

Through trials endured, through joys once known,

The seeds of wisdom are quietly sown.

So cherish each color, both dark and bright,

For shadows give depth to the gift of light.

In life's vast painting, both joy and pain,

Together make beauty that will remain.

Twin Sisters

Poverty and anxiety, twin sisters of strife,

They cut our hearts with a blunt knife.

Not quick the wound, but slow and deep,

A pain that lingers, a grief to keep.

They steal our rest, they haunt our mind,

Peace and comfort, we cannot find.

The future fades, the present cries,

Hope grows dim beneath their skies.

Yet even in shadows, some rise and stand,

With faith as shield and work in hand.

For though twin sisters may tear apart,

They cannot kill the human heart.

And when compassion breaks their reign,

Love and justice heal the pain.

Then life may bloom where want has been,

And hope return to hearts again.

Rev. Dr. Rashid Gill

Uneven Pitch

Some are poor while others are rich,

We are playing but not on an even pitch.

The rules are bent, the dice are thrown,

The game is rigged by hands unknown.

The poor toil hard, yet gain is small,

The rich climb higher, above us all.

Justice falters, fairness hides,

And truth is lost where greed resides.

Yet hope still whispers, quiet, strong,

That right may triumph over wrong.

For even fields can yet be made,

When love and justice lift the shade.

So let us dream, and let us fight,

For equal chance, for human right.

Though some are poor and others thrive,

We seek a world where all may rise.

A Different Song

I'm neither a coward, nor am I strong,

I walk a road where I belong.

For life is vast, and each must see,

A path unique, a destiny.

Some rise as heroes, bold and bright,

Some walk in shadows, far from sight.

Yet each soul sings its fleeting song,

No voice is weak, no voice is wrong.

Life has for everyone a different tone,

A verse to claim, a note their own.

No two the same, yet all entwine,

A chorus shaped by hand divine.

So judge not quickly, nor compare,

For strength takes forms both soft and rare.

The weak, the strong, all play a part,

In life's great song, from heart to heart.

Rev. Dr. Rashid Gill

Bread and Wisdom

Wisdom is more precious than gold,

Its light outshines the tales of old.

It guides the heart, it frees the mind,

A treasure rare, a gift divine.

But wisdom too needs bread to stay,

For hungry souls will lose their way.

The noblest thoughts, the finest art,

Require the strength of body and heart.

The mind may soar, the spirit dream,

Yet life demands its daily stream.

For wisdom fails when hunger cries,

And lofty hopes in silence die.

So let us balance both hand in hand,

The bread of life, the truth so grand.

For wisdom thrives when needs are met,

And shines in lives where hearts are set.

Life's Riddle

Life is a mystery, a riddle untold,

A journey through warmth, through bitter and cold.

Friends and foes appear, both near and far,

And often we're caught in the midst of the spar.

Some offer solace, others betray,

The path winds on, both night and day.

Choices weigh heavy, hearts may fall,

Yet we rise again through it all.

The riddle teaches, if we but see,

That none are purely friend or enemy.

Each holds a lesson, each leaves a mark,

Guiding our souls through light and dark.

So tread with caution, yet walk with grace,

Through tangled webs in life's vast space.

For though the answer may never be known,

The journey itself makes wisdom grown.

Rev. Dr. Rashid Gill

When Fear Surrounds!

When fear surrounds, and doubt is near,

Lift up your heart and face your fear.

The road is tough, the night is long,

But inner strength will make you strong.

Step after step, you'll find your way,

Through darkest night to brightest day.

The winds may howl, the storms may rage,

Yet courage shines through every stage.

No challenge too great, no path too steep,

The seeds of strength are yours to keep.

Believe, endure, let spirit rise,

Your heart holds power beyond the skies.

So walk with faith, stand tall, be brave,

Your inner strength will always save.

Scattered Thoughts

Through every trial, through every spin,

The fiercest courage comes from within.

Rev. Dr. Rashid Gill

A Moment of Peace!

Close your eyes and feel the breeze,

Softly whispering through the trees.

Let the quiet fill your mind,

Leave the troubles far behind.

Hear the river, flowing clear,

Bringing calm to all you fear.

Every heartbeat, gentle, slow,

Life's sweet rhythm starts to grow.

Breathe the stillness, taste the air,

Peace is always present there.

Moments fleeting, yet they stay,

Guiding hearts along their way.

So pause awhile, let silence sing,

Let your soul regain its wing.

Scattered Thoughts

Through the quiet, softly true,

Find the peace residing in you.

Rev. Dr. Rashid Gill

Dreams Take Flight !

Lift your eyes to the endless sky,

Let every dream begin to fly.

Though winds may push and clouds may loom,

Your dreams will rise, and light will bloom.

Step by step, with courage near,

Each little hope will conquer fear.

The world awaits your shining way,

Chase your visions, bright as day.

Never doubt the strength inside,

Your heart can turn the changing tide.

Through every fall, through every fight,

Keep reaching high, your dreams take flight.

So hold your dreams, embrace the sky,

Let every star remind you why.

Scattered Thoughts

The future waits for those who dare,

Your soaring heart can take you there.

Rev. Dr. Rashid Gill

Love Around Us!

Flowing, rhythmic, heartfelt

Love is a river, running wide,

Touching each heart on every side.

In simple smiles, in gentle care,

Love is a song that's everywhere.

Through fleeting moments, strong and true,

It shines in all that people do.

A hand held close, a kind embrace,

Love leaves its mark in every place.

Though time may pass, though paths divide,

Love travels freely, far and wide.

It blooms in hearts, both near and far,

A guiding light, our shining star.

Scattered Thoughts

So let your heart reach out today,

Let love surround you in every way.

Through every life, in all we see,

Love is the bond that sets us free.

Rev. Dr. Rashid Gill

Celebrate Today!

Rise with the sun, greet the new day,

Feel the light, let your spirit play.

Moments of joy are all around,

Listen closely, life's sweet sound.

Dance with laughter, sing with cheer,

Hold close the ones you love most dear.

Every heartbeat, a gift to know,

Life is a river, let it flow.

Take a deep breath, feel the glow,

Celebrate all that helps you grow.

The world is bright, the day is free,

A melody of possibility.

So lift your voice, let gratitude rise,

Let happiness sparkle in your eyes.

Scattered Thoughts

Through every hour, in every way,

Celebrate the gift of today.

Rev. Dr. Rashid Gill

When Fear Surrounds!

When fear surrounds, and doubt is near,

Lift up your heart and face your fear.

The road is tough, the night is long,

But inner strength will make you strong.

Step after step, you'll find your way,

Through darkest night to brightest day.

The winds may howl, the storms may rage,

Yet courage shines through every stage.

No challenge too great, no path too steep,

The seeds of strength are yours to keep.

Believe, endure, let spirit rise,

Your heart holds power beyond the skies.

So walk with faith, stand tall, be brave,

Your inner strength will always save.

Scattered Thoughts

Through every trial, through every spin,

The fiercest courage comes from within.

Rev. Dr. Rashid Gill

A Moment Of Peace!

Close your eyes and feel the breeze,

Softly whispering through the trees.

Let the quiet fill your mind,

Leave the troubles far behind.

Hear the river, flowing clear,

Bringing calm to all you fear.

Every heartbeat, gentle, slow,

Life's sweet rhythm starts to grow.

Breathe the stillness, taste the air,

Peace is always present there.

Moments fleeting, yet they stay,

Guiding hearts along their way.

So pause awhile, let silence sing,

Let your soul regain its wing.

Scattered Thoughts

Through the quiet, softly true,

Find the peace residing in you.

Rev. Dr. Rashid Gill

Dreams Take Flight!

Lift your eyes to the endless sky,

Let every dream begin to fly.

Though winds may push and clouds may loom,

Your dreams will rise, and light will bloom.

Step by step, with courage near,

Each little hope will conquer fear.

The world awaits your shining way,

Chase your visions, bright as day.

Never doubt the strength inside,

Your heart can turn the changing tide.

Through every fall, through every fight,

Keep reaching high, your dreams take flight.

So hold your dreams, embrace the sky,

Let every star remind you why.

Scattered Thoughts

The future waits for those who dare,

Your soaring heart can take you there.

Rev. Dr. Rashid Gill

Love Around Us!

Love is a river, running wide,

Touching each heart on every side.

In simple smiles, in gentle care,

Love is a song that's everywhere.

Through fleeting moments, strong and true,

It shines in all that people do.

A hand held close, a kind embrace,

Love leaves its mark in every place.

Though time may pass, though paths divide,

Love travels freely, far and

Playful, dynamic, uplifting

Rise with the sun, greet the new day,

Feel the light, let your spirit play.

Scattered Thoughts

Moments of joy are all around,

Listen closely, life's sweet sound.

Dance with laughter, sing with cheer,

Hold close the ones you love most dear.

Every heartbeat, a gift to know,

Life is a river, let it flow.

Take a deep breath, feel the glow,

Celebrate all that helps you grow.

The world is bright, the day is free,

A melody of possibility.

So lift your voice, let gratitude rise,

Let happiness sparkle in your eyes.

Through every hour, in every way,

Celebrate the gift of today.

—

Rev. Dr. Rashid Gill

Song of My Soul

You are the song of my soul,

Your touch can make me whole.

In your presence, fears subside,

Like the moon, you calm the tide.

You are the whisper in my night,

A spark that turns my dark to light.

Through every shadow, pain, and ache,

Your love repairs what life may break.

You are the breeze in a heavy air,

A silent prayer, a tender care.

Where my heart falters, you make it strong,

Your essence lingers, soft as song.

Stay with me where dreams unfold,

Warm my spirit when life feels cold.

Scattered Thoughts

For you are the song my soul has known,

The melody that makes me whole.

Rev. Dr. Rashid Gill

Shadows Touch My Heart

Shadows touch my heart,

Tears hide from the start,

Yet my soul will speak,

Strength is what it seeks.

Whispers in the night,

Guiding me to light,

Hope will rise again,

Through the loss and pain.

Though the world feels cold,

Faith makes me bold,

Dreams will find their way,

With each breaking day.

Mountains may stand tall,

Rivers may yet fall,

But my spirit flies,

Beyond the darkest skies.

Rev. Dr. Rashid Gill

My Heart Longs For!

My heart longs to see her, even in a dream,

Yet I am trapped within the world's loud scream.

The night calls her softly, whispers her name,

While shadows of sorrow flicker like flame.

I reach for her light through the veil of despair,

But the weight of the world is too much to bear.

In silence I wander, with tears in my eyes,

Still hoping for morning where her presence lies.

Though storms may surround me, and darkness may gleam,

Her face stays with me, even in a dream.

Heart's Whisper!

My heart beats for you, through the silent night,

Your face lingers softly in the fading light.

Though miles may part us, you're never far,

You shine forever, my guiding star.

I dream of your laughter, gentle and sweet,

A melody that makes my soul complete.

Even in darkness, your warmth I feel,

A love so tender, a bond so real.

The winds may wander, the seas may roar,

Yet my heart will find you evermore.

Through every trial, through every fight,

Your love remains my endless light.

So hold my whisper close in your ear,

A promise of love forever near.

Rev. Dr. Rashid Gill

No distance can fade what our hearts have sown,

My heart beats for you, you're my own.

Dance With Life!

Laugh with the morning, dance with the breeze,

Feel every moment, live with ease.

Joy is a river your soul can know,

Let it flow freely, let your spirit glow.

Sing with the sunlight, run with the streams,

Chase after your wildest dreams.

Every heartbeat a song to play,

A rhythm of life that lights the way.

Lift up your hands, embrace the skies,

Let laughter sparkle in your eyes.

The world is wide, the moments bright,

Celebrate life from morning to night.

So sway with the wind, let worries go,

Feel the magic in every flow.

A heart that dances, a soul set free,

Is the life we were born to be.

Scattered Thoughts

Heart's Whisper!

My heart beats for you through quiet night,

Your eyes still shine with soft and tender light.

Though distance parts us, love will stay,

It whispers softly, never fades away.

I dream of laughter, gentle, sweet,

A melody that makes my soul complete.

Even in darkness, your warmth I feel,

A love so tender, a bond so real.

The winds may wander, the seas may roar,

Yet my heart will find you evermore.

Through every trial, through every fight,

Your love remains my endless light.

So hold my whisper close in your ear,

A promise of love forever near.

No distance can fade what our hearts have sown,

My heart beats for you, you're my own.

Shadows of You

Energetic forward motion, stressed-first

Shadow of you drifts across my day,

Lifts my spirit, guides my way.

Voices of wind call your name,

Flickers of fire, soft flame.

Even in silence, you are near,

Comforting whispers I hold dear.

Your image lingers, everywhere,

A gentle presence beyond compare.

Time may pass and seasons turn,

But my heart continues to yearn.

World may shift, days fade and fly,

Yet your shadow will never die.

When night falls, stars gleam above,

I feel you close, surrounded by love.

A quiet song, tender and true,

Forever entwined in the shadows of you.

Rise Again!

Through the storms that may batter your soul,

Lift your eyes, let the sunlight make you whole.

Every shadow will vanish, you'll see,

The dawn will arrive, set your spirit free.

Take each step with courage, my friend,

Every struggle will someday end.

Though the night may seem endless and long,

Your heart is resilient, brave, and strong.

When doubt presses in, and hope feels small,

Remember the seeds that are planted for all.

Rise from the ashes, let your spirit mend,

The darkest nights will always end.

So lift up your voice, dance in the rain,

Let your courage break through all the pain.

The world is waiting with light so bright,

Rise again, and claim your right.

You Are Never Alone!

Flowing, powerful, dramatic (DUM-da-da)

Tears fall quietly, hearts grow cold,

Love surrounds you, brave and bold.

Step by step, you'll find your way,

Faith will guide you every day.

When shadows linger, fears appear,

Light will chase them, bright and clear.

No trial too heavy, no night too long,

Love carries you steady, keeps you strong.

Wind may howl, and rain may fall,

Yet hope and faith will conquer all.

Lean on the light that never fades,

It leads you through life's shifting shades.

Rev. Dr. Rashid Gill

Walk with courage, hold hearts near,

Feel the whispers of love clear.

Through every challenge, through every tone,

Know in your heart—you're not alone.

Dance With Life!

Laugh with the morning, dance with the breeze,

Feel every moment, live with ease.

Joy is a river your soul can know,

Let it flow freely, let your spirit glow.

Sing with the sunlight, run with the streams,

Chase every shadow, follow your dreams.

Every heartbeat a song to play,

A rhythm of life that lights the way.

Lift up your hands, embrace the skies,

Let laughter sparkle in your eyes.

The world is wide, the moments bright,

Celebrate life from morning to night.

Sway with the wind, let worries go,

Feel the magic in every flow.

A heart that dances, a soul set free,

Is the life we were born to be.

Heart's Whisper!

My heart beats for you through quiet night,

Your eyes still shine with soft and tender light.

Though distance parts us, love will stay,

It whispers softly, never fades away.

I dream of laughter, gentle, sweet,

A melody that makes my soul complete.

Even in darkness, your warmth I feel,

A love so tender, a bond so real.

The winds may wander, the seas may roar,

Yet my heart will find you evermore.

Through every trial, through every fight,

Your love remains my endless light.

So hold my whisper close in your ear,

A promise of love forever near.

Rev. Dr. Rashid Gill

No distance can fade what our hearts have sown,

My heart beats for you, you're my own.

Shadows of You !

Energetic forward motion, stressed-first

Shadow of you drifts across my day,

Lifts my spirit, guides my way.

Voices of wind call your name,

Flickers of fire, soft flame.

Even in silence, you are near,

Comforting whispers I hold dear.

Your image lingers, everywhere,

A gentle presence beyond compare.

Time may pass and seasons turn,

But my heart continues to yearn.

World may shift, days fade and fly,

Yet your shadow will never die.

Rev. Dr. Rashid Gill

When night falls, stars gleam above,

I feel you close, surrounded by love.

A quiet song, tender and true,

Forever entwined in the shadows of you.

Rise Again!

Light, bouncy, uplifting rhythm (da-da-DUM)

Through the storms that may batter your soul,

Lift your eyes, let the sunlight make you whole.

Every shadow will vanish, you'll see,

The dawn will arrive, set your spirit free.

Take each step with courage, my friend,

Every struggle will someday end.

Though the night may seem endless and long,

Your heart is resilient, brave, and strong.

When doubt presses in, and hope feels small,

Remember the seeds that are planted for all.

Rise from the ashes, let your spirit mend,

The darkest nights will always end.

Rev. Dr. Rashid Gill

So lift up your voice, dance in the rain,

Let your courage break through all the pain.

The world is waiting with light so bright,

Rise again, and claim your right.

You Are Never Alone !

Flowing, powerful, dramatic (DUM-da-da)

Tears fall quietly, hearts grow cold,

Love surrounds you, brave and bold.

Step by step, you'll find your way,

Faith will guide you every day.

When shadows linger, fears appear,

Light will chase them, bright and clear.

No trial too heavy, no night too long,

Love carries you steady, keeps you strong.

Wind may howl, and rain may fall,

Yet hope and faith will conquer all.

Lean on the light that never fades,

It leads you through life's shifting shades.

Walk with courage, hold hearts near,

Feel the whispers of love clear.

Through every challenge, through every tone,

Know in your heart—you're not alone.

Dance With Life (Joy & Celebration, Mixed Meter)

Playful, lively, combines iambic and trochaic

Laugh with the morning, dance with the breeze,

Feel every moment, live with ease.

Joy is a river your soul can know,

Let it flow freely, let your spirit glow.

Sing with the sunlight, run with the streams,

Chase every shadow, follow your dreams.

Every heartbeat a song to play,

A rhythm of life that lights the way.

Lift up your hands, embrace the skies,

Let laughter sparkle in your eyes.

The world is wide, the moments bright,

Celebrate life from morning to night.

Sway with the wind, let worries go,

Feel the magic in every flow.

A heart that dances, a soul set free,

Is the life we were born to be.

About The Author

Rev. Dr. Rashid Gill is a poet, author, musician, and visual artist whose work bridges faith, human experience, and creative expression. Born in Lyallpur, Pakistan, he earned his Ph.D. in Theology from Trinity College and University, USA, in 2001.

Before settling in Canada in 1995, Dr. Gill held managerial positions in Saudi Arabia, including Area Manager for Suzuki Motors in Dammam. He now resides in Canada with his beloved wife, Arina Gill, and their three children Rakhshanda Khan, Tabish Gill, and Danish Gill along with four grandchildren.

A prolific writer and insightful thinker, Dr. Gill has authored ten books spanning political essays, Urdu and English poetry, religious reflections, and verse-by-verse biblical commentaries. Among his celebrated works are:

- Merey Loho Qalam (Collection of political articles)
- Sapnou Key Bhanwar (Open verse poetry)
- Midhat Key Phool (Religious poetry)
- Bab-e-Touseef (Religious poetry)
- Namous-e-Ima'an (Verse-by-verse explanation of Prophet Daniel)
- Expounded books of Ecclesiastes and the Gospel of John in Urdu (Under publication)
- 101 Questions Facing Christian (English)
- Shades of Life (Secular poetry in English)

Dr. Gill is also a celebrated music producer, having released multiple CDs including Dast-e-Dua and Dhan Dhan Yesu, as well as later albums blending Christian and secular poetry. His ghazals and jingles have been performed by renowned singers in Pakistan and India, broadcast on Radio Pakistan, and are available on YouTube.

www.ingramcontent.com/pod-product-compliance
Lightning Source LLC
Chambersburg PA
CBHW051206120626
46547CB00013B/1220